New Heinemann Maths

Extension Textbook

Heinemann Educational Publishers
Halley Court, Jordan Hill, Oxford, OX2 8EJ
a division of Reed Educational and Professional Publishing Ltd

Heinemann is a registered trademark of Reed Educational
and Professional Publishing Ltd

© Scottish Primary Mathematics Group 2000

Writing team

John T Blair

Percy W Farren

Myra A Pearson

Dorothy S Simpson

John W Thayers

David K Thomson

First published 2000

05 04 03 02
10 9 8 7 6 5 4 3

ISBN 0 435 17200 X

Produced by Gecko Ltd.
Illustrated by Phil Garner, Shelagh McNicholas,
Lorna Kent and Gecko Ltd.
Printed and bound by Edelvives, Zaragoza.

Contents

1 Copy and complete each sequence.

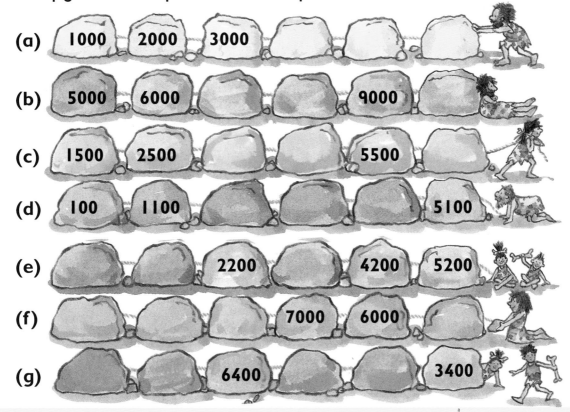

(a) 1000 2000 3000 ___ ___ ___

(b) 5000 6000 ___ ___ 9000 ___

(c) 1500 2500 ___ ___ 5500 ___

(d) 100 1100 ___ ___ ___ 5100

(e) ___ ___ 2200 ___ 4200 5200

(f) ___ ___ ___ 7000 6000 ___

(g) ___ ___ 6400 ___ ___ 3400

2 Count in thousands from

(a) 3800 to 9800   (b) 6300 to 300

3800, 4800

3 Write the number 1000 more than

(a) 2300   (b) 5200   (c) 800   (d) 9000

4 Write the number 1000 less than

(a) 7900   (b) 6400   (c) 10 000   (d) 1500

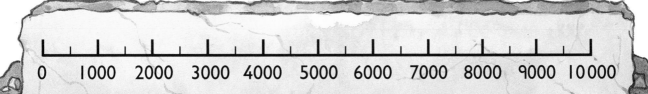

0   1000   2000   3000   4000   5000   6000   7000   8000   9000   10 000

5 What number is halfway between

(a) 2000 and 4000   (b) 5000 and 7000

(c) 10 000 and 8000   (d) 6000 and 4000?

1 Copy and complete each sequence.

(a) 700 | 800 | | | 1100 | |

(b) | 7600 | 7700 | | 7900 |

(c) 3700 | 3800 | | | | 4200

(d) | 4900 | | 5200 | |

(e) 6800 | 6700 | | | 6300

(f) 7300 | 7200 | | | |

(g) | 9900 | 9800 | | | 9500

2 Count in hundreds from
(a) 3200 to 4000 (b) 6400 to 5800

3200, 3300

3 Write the number 100 more than
(a) 2600 (b) 7000 (c) 6900 (d) 9900

4 Write the number 100 less than
(a) 5300 (b) 2000 (c) 10 000 (d) 8100

1000 1100 1200 1300 1400 1500 1600 1700 1800 1900 2000

5 What number is halfway between
(a) 1300 and 1500 (b) 1600 and 1800
(c) 1400 and 1200 (d) 1900 and 2100?

1 Work out each number to find the code to open the safe.

F	A	G	E	B	C	D

To open the safe

A Start at 24. Go back 12 then forward 33.

B Start at 42. Go forward 50 then back 17.

C Start at 36. Go forward 52 then back 8.

D Start at 100. Go back 38 then forward 33.

E Start at 54. Go forward 29 then back 18.

F
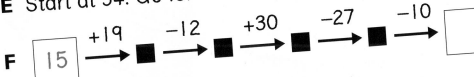

G Find the sum of 28 and 37, minus the difference between 62 and 47.

2 What do you notice about the code numbers?

tøÖ??Î Z

A	D	C	O	L	E	I	R	H	T	N
0	1	2	3	4	5	6	7	8	9	10

1 Find the missing numbers.
Use them to read the Zonk's code.

$2 \times \blacksquare = 16$ $5 \times \blacksquare = 25$ $4 \times \blacksquare = 16$ $10 \times \blacksquare = 40$ $\blacksquare \times 7 = 21$

$\blacksquare \times 2 = 10$ $\blacksquare \times 4 = 0$ $10 \times \blacksquare = 70$ $3 \times \blacksquare = 27$ $5 \times \blacksquare = 40$

$\blacksquare \times 10 = 20$ $4 \times \blacksquare = 32$ $3 \times \blacksquare = 18$ $2 \times \blacksquare = 8$

$\blacksquare \times 5 = 5$ $\blacksquare \times 2 = 14$ $4 \times \blacksquare = 20$ $3 \times \blacksquare = 30$

2

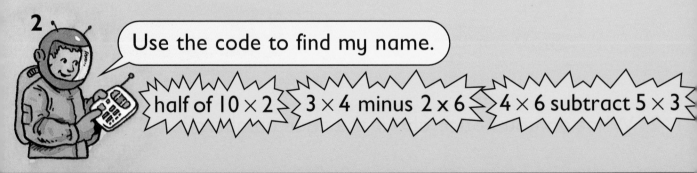

Use the code to find my name.

half of 10×2 3×4 minus 2×6 4×6 subtract 5×3

Children's savings	£20	£10	£5	£2	£1	50	20	10	5	2	1
Max	1	1		1			2	2			
Sue		1	4		2		1	1			5
Roy	1	1		2		1		2		2	1
Mia	1			3		1	1		4		
Cal	1	1			1	4		2	1	2	1

1 How much money has each child saved?

2 Who has **(a)** most notes   **(b)** fewest coins?

3 How much **more** money has
   (a) Max than Sue   **(b)** Mia than Cal?

4 How much **less** money has
   (a) Sue than Cal   **(b)** Max than Roy?

5 How much more money does Sue
   need to save to have a total of £40?

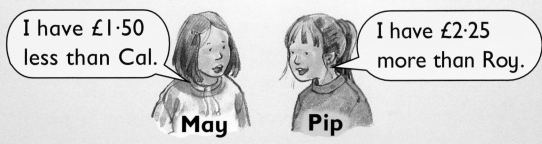

I have £1·50 less than Cal. — **May**

I have £2·25 more than Roy. — **Pip**

6 How much money has **(a)** May   **(b)** Pip?

1 Lisa puts 40p in the collecting tin.
Ken puts in 15p less than Lisa.
Asif puts in the same as
Lisa and Ken together.

How much altogether do the children put in the tin?

2

36 badges

Ken sells one quarter of his badges.
Another eight are broken.
How many badges are left to sell?

3 Lisa and Asif share 5 boxes of pens equally.
How many pens does each have?

10 pens

4

We each have 32 pence.

Charity cards   10p each

Together the children spent 33p
on sweets. They spent the rest
of their money on cards.
How many cards did they buy?
How much did **each** have left?

Connections

A game for 2 or 3 players.

 | 22 + | (20) (28) (41)

 | 60 − | (40) (45) (56)

 | 40 ÷ | (2) (4) (10)

 | 34 + | (8) (16) (50)

 | 21 × | (2) (3) (4)

 | 75 − | (12) (60) (65)

15	50	63	10	4	84
42	10	15	20	50	63
63	20	4	42	84	10
84	42	10	50	20	15
50	15	20	63	42	4
4	63	42	84	15	50

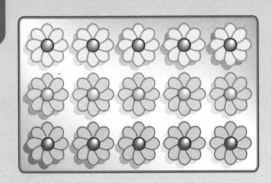
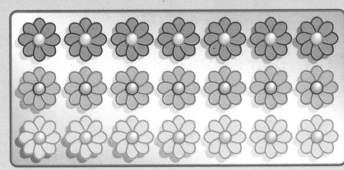

1 (a) $\frac{1}{3}$ of 15   (b) one third of 21

2 (a) $\frac{1}{3}$ of 27   (b) one third of 3   (c) $\frac{1}{3}$ of 30

(d) one third of 12   (e) $\frac{1}{3}$ of 24   (f) $\frac{1}{3}$ of 6

3 (a) Build a tower using 9 cubes.
Make one third of the tower red and
two thirds yellow.
(b) **How many** cubes are • red • yellow?

4 (a) Lay out 18 cubes.
Make one third of the cubes green
and one third blue.
(b) **How many** cubes are • blue • not blue?

5

Two thirds of my cubes are brown.
The other **5** cubes are white.

How many cubes does Sam have altogether?

Sam

1 (a) Divide each tray of fruit equally among 5 people.

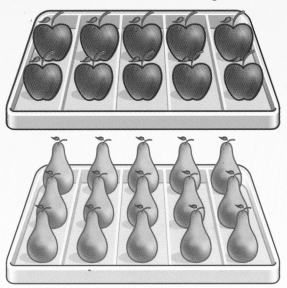
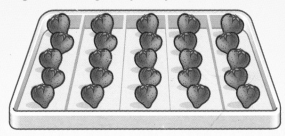
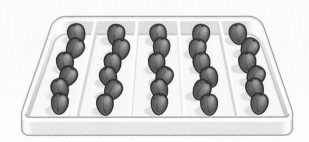

(b) Find one fifth of the fruits on each tray.

(c) What do you notice when you

divide by 5   and   find one fifth ?

2 (a) $\frac{1}{5}$ of 45   **(b)** one fifth of 20   **(c)** $\frac{1}{5}$ of 35

(d) one fifth of 40   **(e)** $\frac{1}{5}$ of 5   **(f)** one fifth of 30

3 Two fifths of the bananas are not ripe. How many fifths **are** ripe?

4 (a) There are 50 apples in a barrel.
$\frac{1}{5}$ of the apples are bad.

How many **fifths** are not bad?

(b) How many **apples** are   • bad   • not bad?

131

252

325

134

117

160

1 How many passengers altogether are carried on the
   (a) red and brown planes   **(b)** blue and orange planes
   (c) green and yellow planes   **(d)** red and blue planes
   (e) brown and orange planes   **(f)** blue and yellow planes?

2 **(a)** $154 + 323$ **(b)** $491 + 208$ **(c)** $230 + 520$
     (d) $505 + 161$ **(e)** $625 + 304$ **(f)** $450 + 347$

Bargain Flights

Amsterdam...£124

Dublin...£103

New York...£230

Sydney...£451

Rome...£162

Paris...£115

3 Find the total cost of flights to
   (a) Amsterdam and Paris
   (b) New York and Rome
   (c) Dublin and Sydney.

4 Which two flights cost exactly £345?

1 How many books altogether were sold on

(a) Monday and Tuesday
(b) Tuesday and Wednesday
(c) Wednesday and Thursday
(d) Thursday and Friday
(e) Friday and Saturday?

Book Sales	
Monday	116
Tuesday	78
Wednesday	215
Thursday	56
Friday	427
Saturday	508

2

(a) 315 + 249
(b) 706 + 106
(c) 335 + 217
(d) 138 + 724

3

(a) 293 + 495
(b) 536 + 81
(c) 154 + 753
(d) 178 + 390

4 How many pages altogether?

(a) 268 pages   329 pages

(b) 344 pages   275 pages

1   For each item find the difference between the old price
    and the **Sale Price**.

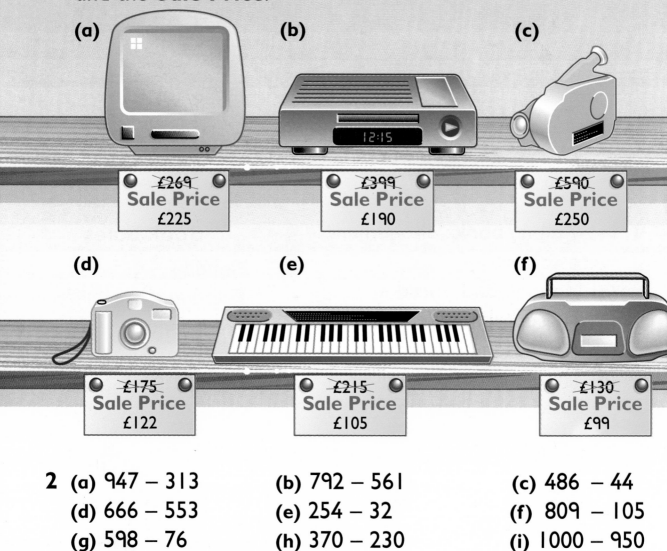

(a)
~~£269~~
Sale Price
£225

(b)
~~£399~~
Sale Price
£190

(c)
~~£590~~
Sale Price
£250

(d)
~~£175~~
Sale Price
£122

(e)
~~£215~~
Sale Price
£105

(f)
~~£130~~
Sale Price
£99

2   (a) 947 − 313   (b) 792 − 561   (c) 486 − 44
    (d) 666 − 553   (e) 254 − 32   (f) 809 − 105
    (g) 598 − 76   (h) 370 − 230   (i) 1000 − 950

3   What is the difference between the **Sale Prices**
    of these computers?

~~£840~~   Sale now half price

~~£995~~   Sale £200 off

Neptune 491 cars

Ocean 57 cars

Dolphin 385 cars

Star 48 cars

Atlantic 164 cars

Princess 273 cars

1 Find the difference between the number of cars carried on the

    (a) *Neptune* and *Dolphin*   (b) *Atlantic* and *Princess*
    (c) *Ocean* and *Atlantic*   (d) *Neptune* and *Princess*
    (e) *Princess* and *Star*   (f) *Ocean* and *Dolphin*

2 (a) $974 - 316$ (b) $540 - 125$ (c) $366 - 127$
   (d) $882 - 623$ (e) $193 - 78$ (f) $770 - 534$

Ferry Prices

Car.........£68
Truck.....£270
Coach....£385
Motor
cycle.......£46

3 How much **more expensive** is the Ferry Price for
    (a) a truck than a car
    (b) a coach than a motor cycle?

4 How much **cheaper** is the price for
    (a) a car than a coach
    (b) a motor cycle than a truck?

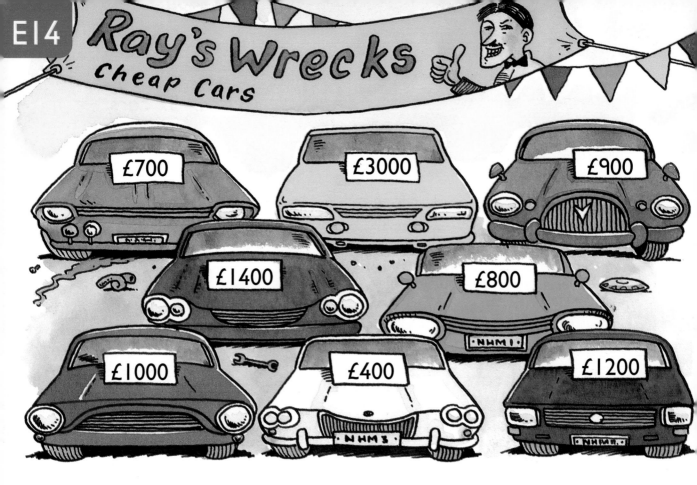

Ray's Wrecks
cheap cars

E14

£700 £3000 £900 £1400 £800 £1000 £400 £1200

1 Find the total price of these cars.

    (a) blue and green   **(b)** white and purple   **(c)** red and blue

    (d) purple and green   **(e)** yellow and red   **(f)** black and white

2 Find the difference in price between these cars.

    (a) black and purple   **(b)** blue and brown   **(c)** brown and white

    (d) white and red   **(e)** red and yellow   **(f)** brown and black

3 Find the difference in price.

    (a)

£1002 £998

    (b)

£996 £1005

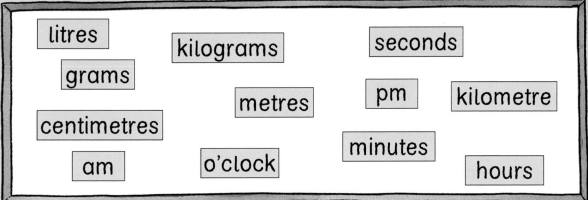

litres
kilograms
seconds
grams
pm
kilometre
metres
centimetres
minutes
am
o'clock
hours

1 Find the missing words.

(a) Jack is about 120 ____ tall.

(b) He weighs about 30 ____ .

(c) The distance from Jack's house to his school is about 1 ____ .

(d) It takes him about 20 ____ to walk to school.

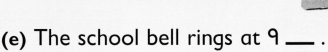

(e) The school bell rings at 9 ____ .

(f) Jack's pet rat weighs about 600 ____ .

(g) Jack drinks about 2 ____ of water each day.

(h) He goes to bed at 8.30 ____ .

(i) His bed is about 2 ____ long.

2 Write four measure sentences about **yourself**.

CAR PARK SPACES
20p for **10** minutes

1 Find the missing entries on the Car Park record.

Car	Enter	Stay	Leave	Cost
P18 ZZB	9.05 am	50 minutes	(a)	(b)
T53 OVL	9.50 am	(c)	11.00 am	(d)
V84 PRN	10.20 am	3 hours	(e)	(f)
M97 WRX	2.00 pm	(g)	(h)	£2·40

2 Find the area, in squares, of each car badge design.

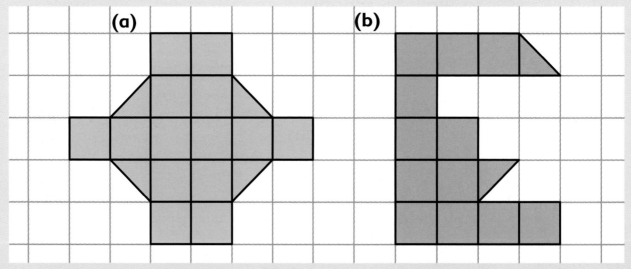

(a)

(b)

3 How many lines of symmetry has each design?

4 Use squared paper.
Draw a design which has some half squares.
Write its area.

1 What am I?

(a) I am half the difference between 500 and 690.

(b) I am double the sum of 46 and 19.

(c) I am five times one quarter of 28.

(d) I am 40 less than 3 times 31.

(e) There are 100 of me in a metre.

(f) There are 500 of me in half a litre.

(g) There are 365 of me in a year.

(h) There are 1000 of me in a kilogram.

(i) I have twice as many sides as a rectangle.

(j) I have five faces. Two are triangles and three are rectangles.

(k) I am the opposite direction to West.

2 Make up some clues of your own to ask a friend.

A –osaur

B –osaur

C –osaur

D –osaur

E –osaur

F –osaur

G –osaur

H –osaur

I –osaur

1 Which dinosaurs
   (a) are blue
   (b) have wings
   (c) do not have spikes
   (d) have spikes and wings
   (e) have wings and no spikes
   (f) have spikes and no wings?

2 Name each dinosaur.

(a)

I am blue.
I have wings.
I have no
spikes.

(b)

I am red.
I have spikes.
I have no
wings.

(c)

I am green.
I have spikes.
I have wings.

(d)

I have spikes.
I have no wings.
I am not red.
I am not green.

3 **(a)** Copy the diagram.
   (b) Draw and colour
   one of the dinosaurs
   in each box.

	spikes	~~spikes~~
red		
~~red~~		

You need coloured shapes.

1 (a) Use **squares** to make patterns like these.

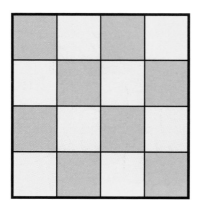
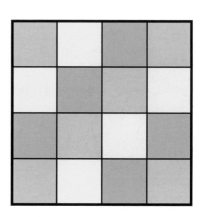

(b) Make your own pattern of squares.

2 (a) Use **rectangles** to make patterns like these.

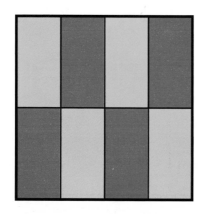
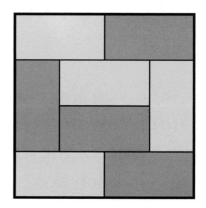

(b) Make your own pattern of rectangles.

1 Use squared paper.

   (a) Copy and continue these patterns.

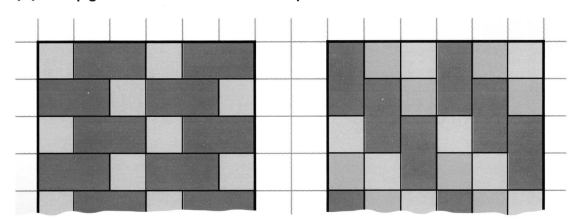

   (b) Draw and colour your own pattern of squares and rectangles.

   (c) Copy and continue these patterns.

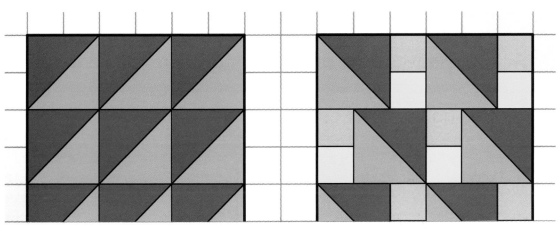

   (d) Draw and colour your own pattern of triangles and rectangles.

2 Use dotty paper.
Copy and continue this pattern of hexagons.

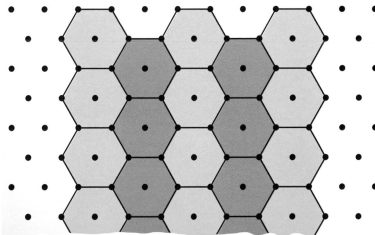

1 Cut out 4 T shapes like this:

2 (a) Place the 4  so that they
fit this shape exactly.

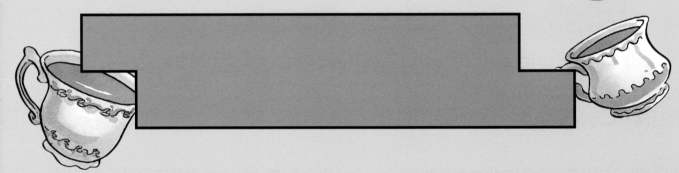

(b) Draw the shape. Show each  using a different colour.

(c) Do all this again for these shapes.